ISBN: 9781764274531

First Edition

Bully Bilby

Pippa Bird

Extended Edition

In the Australian bush, a bilby named Bellamy was known for his mean and pushy behavior. His sharp words and tricks often left his bush friends feeling sad and hurt.

One sunny morning, Bellamy roamed the bush, looking for someone to tease.

He found Cookie quietly sitting by the river and sneered, "Your feathers look scruffy today. And I don't like your laugh."

Cookie's face fell, and he flew away, his usual grin dimmed by sadness and hurt.

Next, Bellamy spotted Pretzel Python clinging nervously to a tree. He pulled roughly on the end of his tail, making him nearly lose his grip.

"You're so clumsy, Pretzel," the bilby mocked.

Pretzel's eyes welled with tears as he slithered higher into the tree, feeling unsafe and scared.

Bellamy ran into Quincy Quokka, who was usually full of cheer. Bellamy shoved him aside, knocking him to the ground where he fell flat onto his back.

"Why are you always so happy? It's annoying," the bilby smirked.

Quincy's smile disappeared, replaced by a frown as he sat alone in the dirt, his spirits dampened.

As the day progressed, Bellamy realized that no one wanted to be around him. He sat under a eucalyptus tree, feeling an unfamiliar pang of loneliness.

Kirri the Calm Kangaroo, noticing
his sorrow, approached him with
a gentle smile.

"Bellamy, why do you look so
sad and alone?" she asked.

Bellamy sighed, "No one wants to play with me. It's hard not to be mean."

"My big brothers were always mean to me, so it just happens. I'm not sure why."

Kirri nodded wisely. "It's hard to break the cycle, Bellamy, but it's not impossible. The first step is to show you're ready to change. Start small. Start with a smile."

Inspired by Kirri's words, Bellamy decided to try. The next morning, he found Warren the Wombat and smiled genuinely.

"Good morning, Warren", he said kindly.

Warren was surprised, but warmly smiled back.

Seeing this, Kirri gathered the other friends to discuss their feelings.

"I know Bellamy's actions are hurtful. How about we think of ways to tell him how we feel?" Kirri suggested.

Cookie spoke up first, "I could tell Bellamy 'I don't like the way you treat me. It hurts my feelings.'"

Pretzel added, "I might say, 'You hurt my body and now I am sad.' It's important he knows his actions have consequences. And that means he can't play with us unless he's nice."

Quincy suggested, "I could say, 'Bellamy we can have more fun together if you're kind. I want to be your friend.'"

Encouraged by Kirri, they all decided to share their feelings with Bellamy.

They approached him together and expressed their emotions honestly.

Bellamy felt ashamed. He hadn't realized how much his actions had hurt them.

"I'm sorry," Bellamy said, his whiskers drooping in sorrow. "I guess I have been mean. Mean is all I know. I am Bellamy Bully Bilby, after all ."

The sad little bilby sighed. "I didn't mean to make you all feel this way. You all deserve to be treated with care and respect."

"I'll try to be a nicer bilby, and a better friend. Please, could you show me how?"

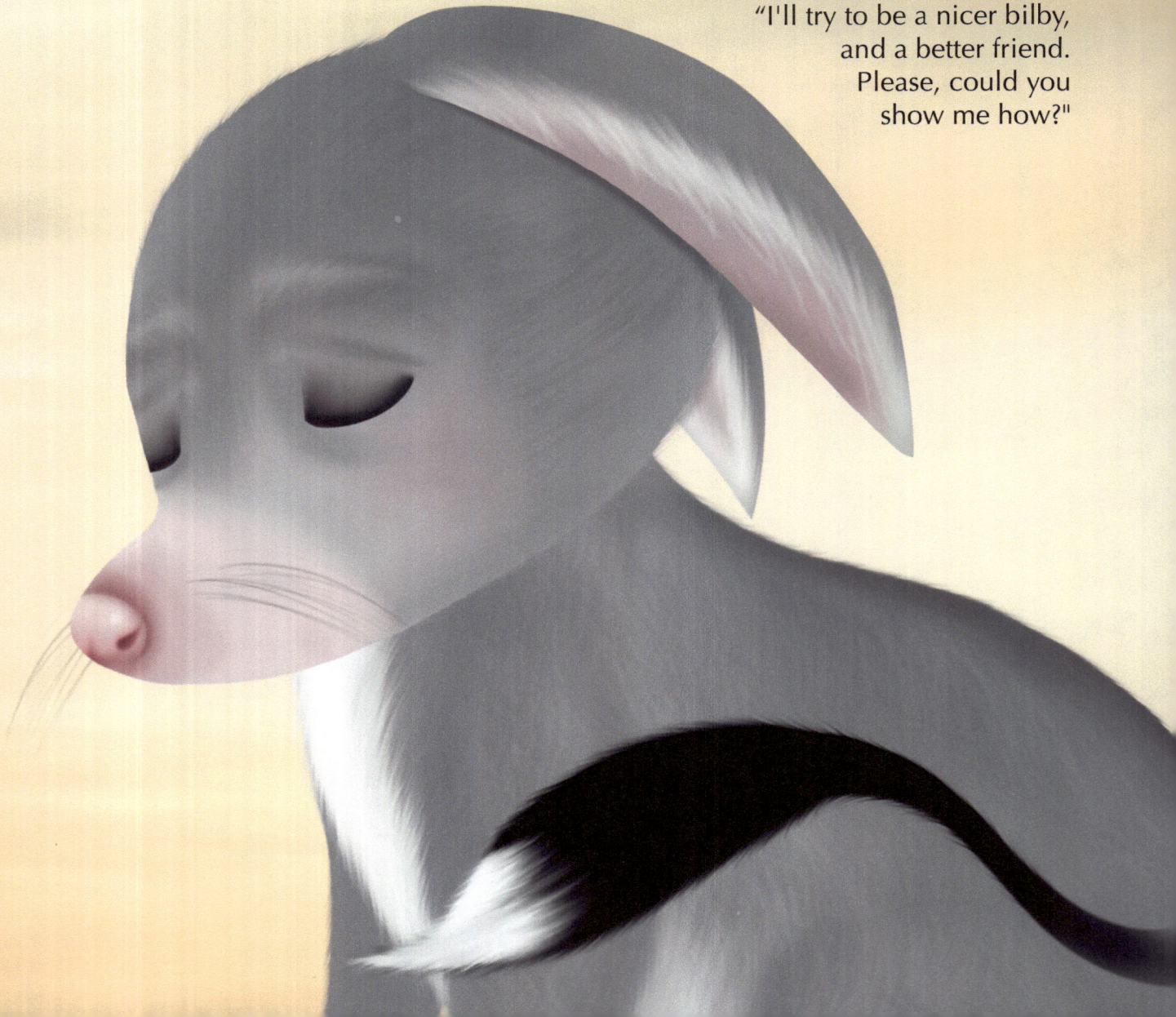

With support and guidance from Kirri and his friends, Bellamy worked hard to change.

He offered genuine compliments, helped out, and, most importantly, he listened.

Over time, his small acts of kindness began to heal the hurt he had caused.

After realizing how much his actions had impacted his friends, Bellamy began to reflect on his behavior.

He remembered how his older brothers had treated him and how their harsh words and actions had made him feel.

Kirri's advice to start small and smile had given him a new perspective.

He didn't want to continue that cycle of meanness.

He knew how it felt to be hurt by others, and he no longer wanted to make his friends feel that way.

Bellamy decided to take more steps to show his friends that
he was sincere about changing. He started by apologizing to
each of them individually.
First, he found Cookie Kookaburra by the river.

"Cookie," he began nervously,
"I'm really sorry for making fun of your
feathers. I think they're actually very
beautiful. And your laugh is my favourite
thing about you."

Cookie looked at Bellamy surprised
by his sincerity. "Thank you, Bellamy. That means a lot. It hurt when you
said those things, but I appreciate your apology. Let's move forward to a
kinder friendship."

Next, Bellamy approached Pretzel Python, who was still wary of him.

"Pretzel, can you please come out so I can talk to you?"

"I'm sorry for pulling your tail and calling you clumsy. I was wrong to do that. You're a great climber. "

Pretzel blinked and slowly nodded. "It's okay, Bellamy. It did hurt, but I'm glad you're trying to change."

Finally, Bellamy went to see Quincy Quokka.
"Quincy, I'm sorry for being rude to you and shoving you. I was
just jealous of how happy you always are."

Quincy smiled warmly.

"Thanks, Bellamy. I appreciate your apology. We can all be happy together if we're kind to each other."

With these heartfelt apologies, the bilby began to mend his relationships with his friends.

Kirri continued to support him, offering advice and encouragement along the way.
(You may finish the story here or continue for further social and emotional learning)

One day, Kirri called a meeting with all the bush friends.

"I think it's important we all support each other," she said. "Let's share more ways we can cope with negative feelings and help each other grow."

Warren the Wombat spoke up first. "When Bellamy used to be mean to me, I felt really sad. But I realized that focusing on my strengths, like my ability to dig, made me feel better."

Penelope the Platypus added, "I started swimming more to clear my mind. It helped me feel less upset and more positive."

Cookie shared his experience. "Practicing self-care, like preening my feathers and spending time with friends who appreciate me, really helped."

Pretzel, said, "Talking to someone I trust, like Kirri, made a big difference. It's important to have someone who will listen."

Quincy Quokka, said, "Focusing on the good things in life and spreading positivity made me feel stronger."

"Helping others also gave me joy."

Kirri smiled at her friends. "These are all wonderful strategies. Remember, it's okay to express your feelings and ask for help when you need it. We're a community, and we should support each other."

Bellamy listened intently to his friends. He realized that everyone had their own way of coping with difficult feelings and that he could learn from them.

Inspired by their resilience, Bellamy made a promise to himself to continue improving and being kind.

Over time, Bellamy's transformation became evident. He helped Warren dig new burrows.

He praised Penelope's swimming skills.

Bellamy admired Cookie's feathers, and supported Pretzel in overcoming his shyness. He even joined Quincy in spreading joy and positivity throughout the bush.

One day, as they all gathered for a bush picnic, Kirri reflected on the changes she had seen. "I'm so proud of all of you," she said. "You've shown that with kindness, support, and communication, we can overcome any challenge."

Bellamy looked around at his friends, feeling a warmth in his heart that he hadn't felt before. He realized that he had found true friendship and happiness through his efforts to change.

And so, the Australian bush became a harmonious place
where kindness reigned, thanks to Bellamy's transformation
and the unwavering support of his friends.

Together, they thrived, creating a community built on
understanding, empathy, and love.

More from this series by Pippa Bird. Available on Amazon.

Calm Kangaroo
Mindfulness Alphabet
Written & Illustrated by Pippa Bird

Quiet Quokka
Written & Illustrated by Pippa Bird

Positive Platypus
Soula's Self-image

Co-regulating Koala
Lost and Found

Unwind with Calm Kangaroo
Written & Illustrated by Pippa Bird

Positive Platypus
Posy's Special Find

Co-regulating Koala
Tumbling Tower

Co-regulating Koala
The Loud Crack

Wobbly Roo

Logical Lyrebird

Hop by Hop
A Gentle Approach to Autism Screening

Hop, Skip, Rest
A Gentle Approach to Understanding ADHD

Elated Emu

Corroborate Cockatoo

Kind Kookaburra

Timely Tarantula

Nonsense Numbat

Polite Python

Calm Kangaroo

Introducing Calm Kangaroo's Mindfulness & Wellbeing Journal: 10 Week Program

Research highlights that mindfulness journaling can significantly improve emotional regulation in primary-school aged children, resulting in better mood stability, reduced anxiety, and stronger self-awareness. This journal is designed to support the same benefits, giving young minds the space to reflect, reset, and grow - one mindful moment at a time.

Baourda, V. C., Brouzos, A., & Vassilopoulos, S. P. (2024). "Feel Good-Think Positive": A Positive Psychology Intervention for Enhancing Optimism and Hope in Elementary School Students. A Pilot Study. International Journal of Applied Positive Psychology, 9(2), 1105-1125.

Devcich, D. A., Rix, G., Bernay, R., & Graham, E. (2017). Effectiveness of a mindfulness-based program on school children's self-reported well-being: A pilot study comparing effects with an emotional literacy program. Journal of Applied School Psychology, 33(4), 309-330.

This delightful adventure invites children to explore mindfulness and self-care with weekly wellbeing check-ins and self-reflections, mindfulness colouring and expressive art activities

Embark on a tranquil journey with our Calm Kangaroo Mindfulness & Wellbeing Journal.

Each day, complete a new task designed to enhance your emotional learning and mental wellbeing. This delightful adventure invites you to explore mindfulness and self-care, accompanied by Calm Kangaroo and her charming bush friends.

The Calm Kangaroo Mindfulness and Wellbeing journal includes a 10 week program to instil emotional intelligence in children aged 8-14. With weekly wellbeing check-ins and self-reflections, mindfulness colouring and expressive art activities, Calm Kangaroo and her bush friends make this an immersive experience with benefits that will last for years to come.

ALULABLU
COUNSELLING SERVICES

70+ Full-colour pages

MINDFULNESS JOURNAL

Age 8-14

Calm Kangaroo
MINDFULNESS & WELLBEING
Journal
10 Week Program

Pippa Bird
BA Psych., DipCouns, M.A.C.A.

Available on Amazon

About the Author
Pippa Bird is a former Mental Health Therapist in Private Practice at Alula Blu Counselling Services, in regional NSW.

Pippa holds a Bachelor in Psychology, a Diploma in Counselling, and a Diploma in Graphic Design, with a primary focus on illustration.

Calm Kangaroo

CALM KANGAROO is a backronym title for a children's mental and emotional well-being program. An initiative designed to educate children about mental health and foster a learning journey of emotional intelligence, resilience and cultivate an open mind through the benefits of reading well-being books, leading to the most important discussions and ideas.

CALM KANGAROO focuses on Curating, Advocating & Leading Mindfulness, & its mission to Kindle Awareness, Nurture Growth, Amplify Resilience, & Orchestrate Open-minds.

www.ingramcontent.com/pod-product-compliance
Lightning Source LLC
Chambersburg PA
CBHW042009080426
42733CB00004B/46

*9 7 8 1 7 6 4 2 7 4 5 3 1 *